The
GIFTS *of*
GOD'S GRACE

Accepting Life as a Gift from God,
Letting God Lead in Good Times and Bad

NANCY TEDFORD OLIVER

authorHOUSE®

AuthorHouse™
1663 Liberty Drive
Bloomington, IN 47403
www.authorhouse.com
Phone: 1 (800) 839-8640

Published by AuthorHouse 10/22/2018

ISBN: 978-1-5462-4872-9 (sc)
ISBN: 978-1-5462-4871-2 (e)

Print information available on the last page.

Any people depicted in stock imagery provided by Getty Images are models,
and such images are being used for illustrative purposes only.
Certain stock imagery © Getty Images.

This book is printed on acid-free paper.

Because of the dynamic nature of the Internet, any web addresses or links contained in
this book may have changed since publication and may no longer be valid. The views
expressed in this work are solely those of the author and do not necessarily reflect the
views of the publisher, and the publisher hereby disclaims any responsibility for them.

King James Version (KJV)
Scriptures were taken from The King James Version of The Bible - Public Domain.

New King James Version (NKJV)
Scripture taken from the New King James Version®. Copyright © 1982
by Thomas Nelson. Used by permission. All rights reserved.

New International Version (NIV)
Holy Bible, New International Version®, NIV® Copyright ©1973, 1978, 1984,
2011 by Biblica, Inc.® Used by permission. All rights reserved worldwide.

To the loving memory of my mother, Lovie Atkins Tedford, the best mother one could ever have. She was a Christian lady and an avid reader of the Word of God, studying her Bible each day and spending hours upon hours searching the scriptures. The Bible was her daily food for the peace of God, which she always had in her life. It was her tool for living this life. She longed to meet Jesus, but she didn't want to leave her children, grandchildren, and great-grandchildren alone to face the world without her strength and prayers.

I told her we'd be okay and would come right behind her. Then days before she went to be with Jesus, she kept telling my sister Peggy and me that there was a light coming from the sky and getting closer to her bedroom window. We looked out the window many times, but we did not see anything. Weeks passed. She had gotten very sick during that time. Peggy took her to the emergency room. My sister-in-law Shirley and I stayed with her that Wednesday night. Mama wasn't able to breathe very well, but during her sickness she was joyfully calling the name of Jesus. He came to her rescue two days later. Yes, even at her death, her concern was for her family, not for herself, because she knew where she was going. Through the faith she had in Jesus Christ, she was going to be with the Father, forever in his arms.

Mama had various writings and could have written many Christian books. There is so much that even her friends did not know about her because she wasn't one who spoke of herself very often. Mama loved to write, leaving her children with her writings as well as her Bibles and the Christian books that she had read many times. Before her death she had written several songs that were recorded locally. In her heart she wanted to spread the

Word of God any way she could. She taught me that life isn't about us but all about God.

Growing up, I remember asking her so many questions. Yes, I was such an inquisitive little girl. She told me she really loved school. In her junior high school years, she made all As in her studies and also assisted her classroom teacher by helping others in her grade and grades below her with their assignments.

I pray that others will be like her, giving their hearts and minds to God, serving him all the days of their lives. America would be a much better place if it would give its all to Christ like our elderly warriors did, not thinking of themselves but thinking of others as Christ did when he died on the cross for all. May my mother's life be a reflection to others so that they, too, walk in the spirit of Christ. *Mama, we miss you.*

CONTENTS

Title Confirmation
and Its Origin

In writing this book, I decided to title it *God's Grace*. Later I was awakened in the night with the thought that the name should be *The Gifts of God's Grace*. I immediately went to my computer changing the title. A gift is *free*. Only the reader can acknowledge the gift or gifts that come from God in each story.

My husband Lanny was reading about the meanings of proper names in the encyclopedia. He came to the name Jane and told me its meaning was "the gift of God." When it came to the meaning of the name Nancy, he read that it meant *grace*. A rush flooded my body from my head to my toes. The two names together gave me the title *The Gift of God's Grace*. This was my confirmation. God did it again. He had spoken, and I believed and received. Through my faith, which was as small as a mustard seed, I believed that God had spoken.

In Matthew 17:20 (KJV), Jesus told his disciples, "If ye have faith as a grain of mustard seed, ye shall say unto this mountain, Remove hence to yonder place; and it shall remove; and nothing shall be impossible unto you."

I found myself trying to make sense of how this book would fit together with the title *The Gifts of God's Grace*. Then it came to me that everything that happens in our lives is a gift of God. We only get through these difficult times by God's grace. If he is there during our hard times, then we know he is there during our good times. God is the giver in all our lives.

Everyone has a testimony. Some make their tests known to other people, while others silently keep these lessons inside their hearts and minds.

Many months into writing this book, I awoke at three in the morning on a rainy July day. I had dreamed it was now time to take this book to press. I knew it would take me some time to finish its editing. Again, I started thinking about its original title and about how I was a gift from God too. You see, my mother was almost forty-eight years old when I was born. It's a miracle I'm even here. I knew I needed to be obedient to God and finish this book. If this book helped just one person, it would have fulfilled its purpose.

This book was written for God's glory. I am only the tool. I pray that it will touch as many lives as possible.

INTRODUCTION

This book of short stories is about the everyday life of your average person—stories of exhortation, encouragement, and learning to rest in God, for he is our inner strength. Any and every situation of life is a gift, a gift of God's grace. God is on our side, but God is leaving the outcome of our battles, our issues, our pain, and our frame of mind to us in order to see what we will do with ours. Trust God, or faint under circumstances and eventually die. The choice is ours.

I wanted to share what strength I drew from happenings, mistakes, and weaknesses in my life. Prayerfully, I tried to pull deep from my inner being a positive outlook by the grace of God to show others how we can turn negative into positive. This book will minister not only to adults in similar situations but also to teens and other younger adolescents. This is a book everyone can understand, and God's Word serves as the explanation.

The Message of Grace

I don't remember this message of grace being taught or preached at the church we attended when I was a child.

My husband, Lanny, often talks of being saved in the Baptist church and what an experience he had when he was saved. I remember the same experience when I was saved. It was such a wonderful feeling, but no one ever told me about God's grace until I met Lanny.

I remember a few words spoken from time to time about grace in the church, but as I look back down memory lane, this word *grace* was hardly ever mentioned in the church my family attended all my childhood.

Lanny's belief in grace, as I have learned in our years of marriage, is such a wonderful thing. Year after year he has talked about God's grace as he understands it according to scripture.

Finally, God gave me the following revelation of grace: Grace is God's free gift to believers. I feel if you are really saved, others will know. You will show it in your daily life. You will give off a light for Christ. I don't believe Grace is a free way to sin. My experience of God's grace is so overwhelming and fantastic that I feel chills running up and down my body and tears of joy in my eyes on a daily basis. This gift is mine, and no one can take it away from me. I have received it in my heart, and now God and I are best friends. God is my joy. He is my life. He loves me, even with my flaws and weaknesses because he knows I walk with him by my side. I can't explain it. No one else can explain it. Each person has to reach this revelation individually. So don't miss your opportunity because it's the most awesome feeling in the world.

In Galatians 1 (KJV), Paul received the revelation of grace through faith. Man did not teach it to him or anyone else.

CHAPTER 1

GOD IS LOVE
FINDING GOD'S GRACE AND ACCEPTING IT

First John 4:16 (KJV) says, "And we have known and believed the love that God hath to us. God is love; and he that dwells in love dwells in God, and God in him."

From as far back as I can remember, my family and I attended a small legalistic church every time the church doors were open. I was saved at age twelve by accepting the Lord Jesus Christ in my heart. At age thirteen I was baptized. My whole life was centered around the church, loving the Lord with all my heart.

There was a lot of good in this church. It was full of God-fearing people who were like family to me, but in my spirit I knew something wasn't exactly right. I had not yet tapped into what it was. My fear of God was terrifying, but I learned in God's Word that God loved us so much that he died for our sins.

Romans 5:8 (KJV) says, "God commended his love toward us, in that, while we were yet sinners; Christ died for all."

As a teenager, I remember thinking I wasn't good enough for God. Even though I loved the Lord and tried really hard to do right, I had a fear within me. *What if I'm not doing enough to be saved?* I wondered.

The teachings at our church were meant to preserve our well-being, but these lessons were very overbearing and taught out of fear instead of love.

After many years I received my revelation from the Lord of this free gift. Through Jesus Christ, I am so very much loved by God, and I have no need for worry because this free gift is eternal in him and through him.

God knows I'm not perfect. No one is. But we are saved through faith in what God's Son, Jesus, did on the cross for all who believe.

Romans 8:1–2 (KJV) says, "There is therefore now no condemnation to those that are in Christ Jesus, who walk not after the flesh, but after the Spirit. For the law of the Spirit of life in Christ Jesus hath made me free from the law of sin and death."

I loved reading my Bible, but one day when I was around the age of twenty-five, I started studying the Bible for myself along with my mother, learning this God of legalism, a God we all feared so much. This God, which I had been taught all my life, was not in alignment with God's Word about who he really was. I discovered God's love and grace.

This good news about God's free gift can be received by faith through Jesus Christ

Romans 3:23–28 (KJV) says,

> For all have sinned and come short of the glory of God; Being freely justified by his grace through the redemption that is in Christ Jesus. Whom God hath set forth to be a propitiation through faith in his blood, to declare his righteousness for the remission of sins that are past, through the forbearance of God; to declare, I say, at this time his righteousness: That he might be just, and the justifier of him who believes in Jesus. Where is boasting then? It is excluded. By what law?

of works? Nay: but by the law of faith. Therefore we conclude that a man is justified by faith without the deeds of the law.

These following scriptures gave me more insight into God's free gift:

Romans 5:19–21 (KJV) says,

> For as by one man's disobedience (speaking of Adam) many were made sinners, so by the obedience of one (speaking of Jesus) shall many be made righteous. Moreover, the law entered, that the offense might abound. But where sin abounded, grace did much more abound; that as sin hath reigned unto death, even so might grace reign through righteousness unto eternal life by Jesus Christ our Lord.

John 3:16 (KJV) says, "For God so loved the world that he gave his only begotten son, that whosoever believeth in him should not perish, but have everlasting life."

As you follow me through my story, I will show you who God is along with scripture. He says he is "a God of love." God wants you and me to have good lives. He loves us. You know how you hurt when your child hurts? Well, God hurts even more when we hurt. He's not out to get you, but he came, bled, and died so that we might enjoy our lives. He has given us eternal life.

First John 4:8 (KJV) says, "He that loves not knows not God; for God is love." This scripture did not say that God is *as* love or *like unto love* but that God *is* love. We need to receive this revelation.

First Corinthians 13:4 (KJV) says, "Charity (love) suffers long and is kind." First Corinthians 13:8 then says, "Charity (love) never fails." So as we put these messages together, we learn that God never fails, that God suffers long, and that God is kind.

He gave up his Son on the cross for all the world, and this act of kindness should be an eye-opener. *Wake up. Look up. Believe.* What more does God need to do. The Word of God is so clear and detailed about how we need to cast our care onto God and accept him for who he says he is.

Psalm 55:22 (KJV) says, "Cast your cares on the Lord and he will sustain (keep) you; He will never let the righteous fall."

Chapter 2

Trusting God
Learning from Those around You

Because I was not taught of God's love, I did not develop a trust in God as I needed. Let me continue to tell you what happened in my life that awakened the trust I was missing.

I was driving with my granddaughter Kelsey (age three) sitting in her car seat in the back of my vehicle. All was quiet. Then suddenly, she cried out to me, "Nona, you must trust God." I immediately started crying and thanking God for speaking through this child. I had been going through a battle in my mind, but no one knew.

Five years passed. I was at the same granddaughter's house. She said, "Nona, I have something to show you." I looked, and I saw it was a rock about the size of her hand. She had beautifully painted it and was going to use it as a paperweight. She had written on it, "Trust God." I knew at that point that this message was directed again to me.

I had not been trusting God the way I should have. I had been worrying, trying to figure out answers to problems, issues, and questions. I had not given it all completely to God. I thought I was trusting, but I wasn't. God sent this child to me twice. I finally got it! Sometimes we think that we have given it all to God, but we are still carrying the load.

I learned that accepting the inner peace that God had given me would take me to heights I had never explored or never would explore without it. And here it was again. By his grace I knew it would be possible for me to trust him.

Matthew 11:29–30 (KJV) says, "Take my yoke upon you, and learn of me; for I am meek and lowly in heart: and ye shall find rest unto your souls. For my yoke is easy, and my burden is light."

CHAPTER 3

A Personal Relationship with Jesus Christ through Prayer, Praise, and Meditation

I came to the realization I was not meditating on God's Word enough. To grow in God's Word, we have to eat and digest the Word just like we have need to eat and digest our natural food so that we can remain healthy and stay alive.

I learned first to pray and then to praise and then to meditate while listening to what God was saying. I would let the peace of God reign in my heart. I learned how powerful praise was to God. Praise glorifies God, and this is our duty to God.

I then remembered my mother's favorite scripture. Philippians 4:7–8 (KJV) says,

> And the peace of God, which passes all understanding, shall keep your hearts and minds through Christ Jesus. Whatsoever things are true, whatsoever things are honest, whatsoever things are just, whatsoever things are pure, whatsoever things are lovely, whatsoever things are of good report; if there be any virtue, and if there be any praise, think on these things.

I've learned many important things about being a servant for Christ and keeping a servant's heart. I came to believe in the realness of my salvation, and no one—not my pastor or my friends—could give me this revelation. It took me looking unto Jesus to find answers about my faith in him.

One morning a few years back, I awoke from sleeping, remembering a scripture I was given in my sleep. Isaiah 60:2 (KJV) says, "But the Lord shall rise upon thee, and his glory shall be seen upon thee. By reading this scripture I learned that how I see myself determines my attitude toward life. For strength in Jesus, to obtain this confidence, peace and love for oneself, we must come into the presence of God."

Staying close to God through abiding in his presence will help us live our cause so that he is able to use us for his benefit.

I knew that reading the Word of God and praying daily was important to do each day. I was so encouraged by knowing that through prayer, praise, and meditation, everyone could have a close relationship with Jesus Christ. I had learned that trials and temptations brought me to prayer, which in turn brought me closer to God. Meditation and praise along with this prayer brought me into a place of complete peace. I felt that reading and studying God's Word along with praising and meditating was a vital part of life that I learned from writing this book. All was a gift from God (a gift of God's grace).

Chapter 4

Being a Spirit-Filled Believer by Hearing God through His Word

Being a Spirit-filled believer means being filled to the brim with God's Spirit, totally believing and trusting in the hope of one's calling.

It took me awhile to fully give myself over to the Spirit of God that abides inside me, believing, knowing, and fully hoping that I had been made whole through my faith. I was forever accepted into his spiritual kingdom. I was accepted through the faith he had given me, a faith earned only by his love and grace.

Ephesians 3:16–17 (KJV) says, "That he would grant you, according to the riches of his glory, to be strengthened with might by his Spirit in the inner man; That Christ may dwell in your hearts by faith; that you being rooted and grounded in love."

Luke 12:32 (KJV) says, "Fear not little flock, for it is your Father's good pleasure to give you the kingdom."

God loves us so much. In this scripture he's telling us not to fear, for his kingdom is ours now. He tells us that our eternal life started when we accepted him in our hearts and believed him for who he says he is and what he says he will do. He has proven this in the scriptures.

I was again beckoned to search the scriptures. John 5:39 (KJV) says, "Search the scriptures; for in them you think you have eternal life, and these are they which testify of me."

I then realized what he was saying. We can look into the Word of God and truly find exactly who he is, given to us by revelation of his Spirit, that is within all who believe."

Galatians 5:16 (KJV) says, "Walk in the Spirit and you will not fulfill the lust of the flesh." This scripture alone tells us how to walk with God. To learn to be spiritually minded instead of being driven by the flesh. And with our strong belief in Jesus through his Word, accepting the grace he has given us, we can overcome.

Hebrews 4:16 (KJV says, "Let us therefore come boldly unto the throne of grace, that we may find mercy and grace to help in time of need (to help in our time of need)."

CHAPTER 5

JESUS IS THE ONLY WAY TO GOD
NOT OF WORKS LEST ANY MAN SHOULD BOAST

Some might think in their hearts that they will get into heaven when they die because they were good on earth. No, that won't do it. The blood of Jesus Christ is the only way to God.

Good works, such as tithing, giving donations for a worthy cause, volunteering, being nice, keeping the rules of the land, or doing good deeds, won't get you there. These are good and needed. Works can help, but these are not salvation (the saving of a soul).

Believing Jesus died on the cross for your sins, asking God for forgiveness through Jesus Christ, and inviting him to live in your heart is salvation. By the blood of Jesus, salvation is possible. Then it's a faith walk.

Ephesians 2:8–9 (KJV) says, "For by Grace are you saved through faith; and that not of yourselves: it is the gift of God; not of works, lest any man should boast."

Chapter 6

Motive
Life Is Not about Us

We are to be used for the glory of God, not our glory. Our glory is vain glory. God's glory is eternal life. You must have a heart for God.

I asked myself, "What is your motive?" We will only receive a reward for good works if we are motivated to give God *all* the glory for these works. I realized at this point, that I now had learned how to give God all the glory from my heart. I thought about all the years I had thought I was giving God all the glory, but I learned I had not been. I loved the Lord and grew up in the church from the time I was a baby, and I went to church every time the church doors opened. I was very active in church from age twelve. I worked as the children's choir leader, a believer on the worship team, and the assistant to the youth pastor, praying every day for God to express his way with my life. God was now showing me the truth. I had thought of myself too much. I was pleasing a man rather than doing it all for God. I knew *all* was the keyword (all to God). First Corinthians 10:31 says, "So whether you eat or drink, or whatever you do, do it all for the glory of God."

I knew now what God needed and wanted from me. I had to stop thinking of myself and instead think of him only, lifting him up. It's not about me, but it's all about him.

Acts 13–22b (KJV) says, "King David was a man after God's own heart." Although he had many flaws, God used them for his good because King David had a heart for God. He was repentant and humble toward God (pitiful). King David always surrendered his life to God, learning from his own mistakes.

It took some time for King David to learn that life wasn't about him. But when he finally learned, then God was gracious, forgiving him and giving those ungodly things that David had done good endings. This would have never happened if David had not gotten his priorities in order.

God does want us to enjoy the fruit of our labor and to enjoy life, but some get caught in a trap and think, *Well, it's my life!* No, it's not your life! We are here for a purpose. What is our purpose? Why are we here? God loves us so much that he gave us life, and he died for us so that we could be saved. If we don't know our purpose, then we should seek God for it.

Before Jesus went to the cross, he was praying to the Father. John 12:27b (KJV) says, "Jesus said, 'But for this purpose I came to this hour.'"

Your purpose might be as simple as the following scripture: "Whatsoever your hand finds to do, do it with all your might" (Ecclesiastes 9:10a KJV).

You might be used by God in certain areas—helping in the church, helping an elderly lady cross the street, praying in your closet for others, coaching a little league baseball team, baking cake for the sick, and/or taking up the offering. Then again, you might be called to be an ambassador for Christ, a teacher, a pastor, or maybe even an evangelist.

Life is short, so we need to start doing what we are called to do. One calling is as important to God as the other. We are one body in Christ, and it takes all the parts to make a complete body. You might be the little finger or even the fingernail, and others might be the eyes, the hands, or the arms; however, that's okay. All have their part to play in this body of Christ. Each has his or her own work to do.

Romans 12:4–8 (KJV)

> For as we have many members in one body, but all the members do not have the same function, so we, being many, are one body in Christ, and individually members of one another. Having then gifts differing according to the Grace that is given to us, let us use them. If prophecy, let us prophesy in proportion to our faith; or ministry, let us use it in our ministering; he who teaches, in teaching; he who exhorts (giving advice) in exhortation; he who gives, with liberality (generously); he who leads, with diligence (carefully); he who shows mercy, with cheerfulness.

Once again, I learned that my motive needed to be right before God. I need to live for him, letting him guide and lead me in the direction I need to go.

Matthew 5:16 (KJV) says, "Let your light so shine before men, that they may see your good works, and glorify your Father which is in heaven."

CHAPTER 7

DELIVERANCE FROM FRUSTRATION THROUGH GOD'S LOVE

As a young Christian girl, my frustration with so-called Christians and also evildoers was great. I have learned along the way that the presence of hypocrites in the church is one of the main reasons some people do not attend.

I remember one of the leaders of our church told me she had not read her Bible in weeks. As a teenager, I always read my Bible. I couldn't understand that she was not reading her Bible. But I was self-righteous, and I should not have been. But given what I had been taught, I had developed this thought pattern—that is, until God brought me out. Of course, she should have been reading and studying the Word, but God is her judge. God sees everyone's heart. The human heart is not visible through human eyes unless God reveals it. I knew I needed to show mercy. Matthew 5:7 (KJV) says, "Blessed are the merciful: for they shall obtain mercy."

I learned from this that no one is saved through his or her righteousness but by our faith through God's grace. Isaiah 64:6 (KJV) says, "Our righteousnesses are as filthy rags."

I had been trying to figure things out on my own, but finally, I gave it to God, knowing that I had put my trust is him. I knew that any hardship or roadblock would only make me stronger because I had committed my life to God and trusted him with my whole heart. We are entirely in his hands, even though sometimes it seems he has forsaken us. Those are the times when God is carrying us. Without him, we have no strength. Through him we are most powerful, even when it looks like we are at our weakest. We serve an awesome God.

CHAPTER 8

BONDAGE OR GRACE

As a child, I was taught to focus on so many unnecessary rules in the church. Without the proper focus, I did not get the chance to enjoy life as a regular teen in a Christian church. Over the years my pastors taught me as they felt they needed to, but this free message of grace was never mentioned.

I was a good teenager, but I did not get a chance to enjoy this Spirit-filled freedom. Many are still confused because of ignorance and the many untruths they've been taught. God-fearing people are being taught that God said this or that, or they are told what God wants. These teachings have been passed from one generation to another. In these strict legalistic churches, many just give up. Satan comes to them because of their low self-esteem. They often think, *I may as well sin and keep on sinning because the preacher or teacher said I was on my way to hell because I cut my hair, because I'm wearing pants, or because I'm wearing makeup.* Such teachings are untrue. There are and have been many people with good hearts that God wanted to use. God has given them talents; however, through these teachings, their confidence in themselves and in God is torn down, and they just quit trying to do the right thing. Satan fools them into thinking that God requires too much of them, that God's expectations are just too high. At that point, they are destroyed not only spiritually but emotionally and sometimes physically. They may sink into heavy drinking or worse. I tried to separate this bondage from the love of God.

I was sitting in a restaurant when I noticed a young girl walking down the aisle. She had no smile, no expression. I could feel her fear. I wanted to tell her what I had learned through my life's journey, that bondage is not peaceful and it is the fear of people, not the fear of God.

I then was taken back with thoughts of my childhood, thoughts of bondage that our church taught when I was a child. I remembered the pain and fear I had to face every day of my life. The leaders of our church were sincere, teaching their assembly to live separately from school friends and any other person they felt might be worldly (of the world) because they did not hold the same belief or religion. I gave up friends, sports, school plays, and other activities. I was never really the teenager I wanted to be, the adolescent who could build great memories with school friends.

I have learned to look on the positive side of my situation, *and there was a positive side.* I was a virtuous young girl. I was honest, and I did my best to do the right thing. I thank God for that.

As I have studied the scriptures through my life, I now know the difference between a free gift and bondage. The following scriptures helped me on my journey to find God's love and grace:

Romans 8:15 (KJV) says, "For you have not received the spirit of bondage again to fear; but you have received the Spirit of adoption, whereby we cry, Abba, Father (having a son/daughter relationship with Christ)."

First John 4:18 (KJV) says, "There is no fear in love; but perfect love casts out fear: because fear hath torment. He that fears is not made perfect in love."

John 5:24 (KJV) says, "Jesus said, 'He that hears my word and believeth on him that sent me hath everlasting life, and shall not come into condemnation; but is passed from death unto life.'"

Romans 13:10b (KJV) says, "Love is the fulfilling of the law. We are saved through God's love in what Jesus did on the cross for all."

Second Corinthians 5:21 (KJV) says, "He hath made him (speaking of Jesus Christ) to be sin for us, who knew no sin; that we might be made the righteousness of God in him."

I know that we cannot impress God with works. He paid the cost. All we need to do is confess our sins, accept him in our heart, and believe. There's no need for fear. It's that simple.

If we are truly saved, we will follow Jesus Christ and will continue to press on toward our higher calling.

CHAPTER 9

CHRISTLIKE COMPASSION

I always rode the school bus back and forth to school. It was an hour ride each way. I usually sat toward the front of the bus because the kids in the back could be so loud and annoying. I had noticed a girl who was slightly younger than me who rode each day. She was a beautiful yet very poor and seemingly sad girl who always looked down as she walked. She had no friends, and she usually sat alone. Her clothes were soiled and wrinkled. As she would get on and off the bus each day, you could see that her home was very rundown. I thought she might be a mistreated child, but I never knew for sure. I felt so much compassion for her, and I asked her to come home with me so that I could clean her up and perhaps talk with her. I wanted to tell her she needed to have more confidence and self-worth.

The evening she got off the bus with me at my home, I gave her several outfits from my closet. I ran her a bath and gave her soap. Afterward, she looked like a different person. I showed her how to hold her shoulders up and to walk with confidence. She smiled. I will never forget the feeling that helping her gave me. I had brought this smile to her face.

The next year I noticed her getting on the bus with confidence, all clean, and actually excited about going to school. I saw she now had friends, and she talked with them all the way to school and back home.

When God gave us grace, all the fruits of the spirit were wrapped up in it. We should show compassion for others and try our best to show all the fruits of the spirit which are obtained through God's grace.

God has given us grace to love the unlovable, to care for the rebellious, to pray for our enemies, to help the needy, and to strengthen the weak.

He is in us, and he needs us to fully surrender our lives to him. Galatians 5:22–25 (KJV) says, "The fruit of the spirit is love, joy, peace, longsuffering, gentleness, goodness, faith, meekness and temperance: against such there is no law. And they that are Christ's have crucified the flesh with the affections and lusts. If we live in the Spirit, let us also walk in the Spirit."

Although I was just a child, this compassion I felt came from God. It was a gift from God.

CHAPTER 10

JESUS IS THE GOOD SHEPHERD
THE MESSAGE OF LOVE

John 10:11 (KJV) says, "Jesus said, 'I am the good shepherd: the good shepherd gives his life for the sheep.'" I was meditating on this scripture in which Jesus gave up his life for us. He proved his love for us by dying for our sins. He gave up his life so that we might live. I kept thinking about how we really do have the strength through Christ to love the unlovable.

I dreamed I was in a room among a church choir filled with people who were supposed to be saints of God. I had joined this choir. Each person in the choir told me in a mean way that they did not need me in the choir. I kept speaking to them all, and I got the same response from everyone there. Their attitudes were haughty. I started crying, and I told them that we should love one another. I knew it wouldn't be an easy thing to be in this choir. I felt God was telling me I needed to continue preaching this message of love.

In my heart, I felt this love God has bestowed to us and through us. All we need to do is believe and accept it. Discouragement comes from Satan, and we should be so full of God that there is no room for doubt, torment, or fear. I knew that this gift of love from God was given to all. We should be so encouraged. First Corinthians 13:4, 8 (KJV) says, "Love suffers long … Love never fails."

Second Corinthians 5:17 (KJV) says, "If any man be in Christ, he is a new creature: old things are passed away: all things are become new. All things are of God, who hath reconciled us to himself by Jesus Christ, and hath given to us the ministry of reconciliation." This passage goes on to say, "For he hath made him (speaking of Jesus) to be sin for us, who knew no sin; that we might be made the righteousness of God in Him."

CHAPTER 11

STRENGTH THROUGH ADVERSITY

For years I watched my husband Lanny live for the Lord, trying to do the right thing in every aspect of his life. He was active in the church and loving every minute of his walk with Christ.

In 1998, I had a dream about Lanny. It seemed that I was always dreaming. Sometimes I would tell others of these dreams. Whether they believed me or not, I don't know. But sometimes my dreams would come to pass.

Acts 2:17 (KJV) says, "In the last days, God says, I will pour out my spirit on all people. Your sons and daughters will prophesy, your young men will see visions, your old men will dream dreams."

In my dream Lanny had been in an accident. I looked at him and saw that he only had one arm and no legs. He walked with a crutch. I knew it was impossible for him to walk with a crutch since he now only had one arm and no legs.

Then one year later, it happened!

Late one night Lanny and I read the Bible and then prayed for our children and family. Lanny went to sleep with the Bible lying open on his chest. The phone rang and woke us up. I answered the call. We rushed to the hospital.

The news would try Lanny as a believer in Christ. Something so devastating had happened that even more than a decade later as I am writing this book, Lanny still can't shake it.

His teenage son had died. Dusty, who was only seventeen, had been in an auto accident. This terrible happening would bring Lanny to his knees in every way. He felt depressed with no hope or understanding. He always asked, "Why, Lord?" He was full of questions but had no answers. This caused Lanny to withdraw. He had no earthly or spiritual interest in anything, not our marriage, family, church, or friends. Only God knew his sadness. I felt his pain, our pain, the desolate feeling, the loneliness, the darkness. I knew he was trying to trust God in this, but this feeling of anguish and mistrust would last for years. No one in our church seemed to understand. Some would try to understand. We knew that no one could really understand unless they had been through it themselves.

As time passed, Lanny and I felt as if we lived on an island. We were totally alone, except for God. Then I thought about the time when John was on the island of Patmos and received the book of Revelation. My alone time had given me the words to write this book.

When he wasn't working, Lanny would come home and throw himself into watching sports on television. He didn't have much contact with people. During this time we hardly ever went anywhere together. We didn't have any close friends except for some family members.

Even though Lanny did not talk about it much in our daily lives, I always knew he was hurting. I knew that it would take some time to heal. This sad thing had happened for a reason.

As Lanny pressed on toward believing in God with no understanding of his reasons, I felt God would bring him through triumphantly. I knew God had a purpose for him that would be so powerful, and Lanny would be able to complete this work through his great loss.

Romans 8:28 (KJV) says, "And we know that all things work together for the good to them that love God, to them who are the called according to his purpose."

There was one thing I felt I knew about Lanny, namely that he loved God. At first, Lanny feared for Dusty's soul. Lanny knew Dusty had accepted Jesus into his heart as a child; however, he had not been attending church regularly, and most of Dusty's friends did not attend either. But God did not forsake Lanny through this. God knew something we didn't know. God knew Dusty's heart. The phone rang. It was Lanny's sister Angie. She found many things in Dusty's school locker that helped us realize of where his eternal soul was. Yes, Lanny learned many things about Dusty. Angie found many things Dusty had written. He wrote about how God was like a dad to him. He also wrote about family and friends. I knew that this was God's way of allowing Lanny to put Dusty to rest with peace so that he could go on living this life without Dusty. God had a plan. I knew Lanny would eventually gain strength through adversity.

Sometimes we withdraw from God when bad things happen to us. But he will not leave or forsake us. He is always there if we will reach out to him. We, God's elect, have a covenant with him that cannot be broken.

Deuteronomy 4:31 (KJV) says, "For the Lord thy God is a merciful God; he will not forsake thee, neither destroy thee, nor forget the covenant of thy fathers which he swear unto them."

CHAPTER 12

How Do I Know I Love God?

I kept asking myself, "How do I know I love God? How do I know I love him enough?" I knew I was not perfect and that I depended on his grace for perfection.

I felt I loved God, but I kept asking myself those questions. I started studying the love I was supposed to feel for God. I knew Jesus died for us because he loved us. But how was I supposed to be content with knowing I loved him enough? I pondered this question many times day after day, night after night. I wanted an answer so that I could feel perfect peace. In my spirit I could hear God saying to me, "It's all about yours and my relationship."

I took my Bible and prayed that God would give me this revelation through the scriptures, as he had given me revelation so many times before about other questions. I found that God is the only perfect one.

Romans 5:5b (KJV) says, "God has poured out his love into our hearts by the Holy Spirit, whom he has given us. To clarify; our love is only perfect through him."

Christ shed his love abroad in our hearts when we accepted him as our Lord and Savior. This love is enough. We draw closer to him with the decisions we make in our lives to obey him, and there is no separation in this.

First John 1:9 (KJV) says, "If we confess our sins. He is faithful and just to forgive us our sins and to cleanse us from all unrighteousness."

As I continued to search the scriptures, I learned that if we were of a repentant heart, even if we made sinful mistakes, God would forgive faithfully. Then I knew that Satan could not separate us from God.

Romans 5:11 (NKJV) says, "We rejoice in God through our Lord Jesus Christ, through whom we have received reconciliation."

Romans 8:38–39 (KJV) says, "Neither death, nor life, nor angels, nor principalities, nor powers, nor things present, nor things to come, nor height, nor depth, nor any other creature, shall be able to separate us from the love of God, which is in Christ Jesus our Lord."

By God's Word, we can find any answer we need if we seek it. Through scripture, once again God had shown me his love and my love for one another.

CHAPTER 13

FULLY BELIEVING JESUS IS WHO HE SAYS HE IS

The only way we can have faith in Jesus is by the grace of God. With this grace, all things are possible, and we can only receive this faith by his grace. One might brag about his or her surmounting faith, but we can't have faith unless it's given to us by God's grace. Yes, faith, too, is a gift from God. So you see, it's like Mama always said, "It's all in God." We're nothing without him.

In my walk with Christ throughout the years, people would ask me, "How do you know that Jesus is real?" Let me tell you a story that amazed me and my family.

On day I got a pain in my chest. Lanny drove me to the medical center. After I was diagnosed with a viral infection, the doctor wrote a prescription for the pain and sent me home. I took the medicine but grew sicker. I remember being so sick that I thought I was going to die. I prayed that God would heal me. When Lanny came home from work that afternoon, I was in the bed with the bedroom door locked. He finally got into the room and woke me up. I was sweating, and I seemed really out of it. I remember walking on white feathers toward a stairway that was covered with white feathers too. As I approached the stairs, three men dressed in white tucks and wearing white top hats were marching toward me. The taller man was in the front, the second tallest behind him, the third (shortest) behind him. Each marched in perfect unity, the one behind the other. When I looked up, I saw two dark figures fly to the men dressed in white. I heard the men dressed in white say, "You can't have her. She belongs to us." The dark figures flew away. I knew I was going with the men in white. I remember I felt completely at peace, not worrying at all.

Whether it was all a dream, a vision, or a near-death experience, I do not know. I remember walking in the living room where Lanny was and telling him that I thought I had died. Lanny took me back to the doctor. They x-rayed my chest and found out that I had pneumonia. In a little more than a week, I was fine. I have always known that this happened for a reason. I know God healed me.

God taught me through this that my eternal life starts today, so close to my step into eternal life. I should never be afraid, for I am always sheltered in the arms of God. I now am assured that he has us in the palm of his hand.

My story is confirmation that God is real. He is who he says he is. This is a confirmation not only to the doubtful and the unbelieving but to others who need encouragement.

CHAPTER 14

FORGIVING YOURSELF

Through life's journey I've seen family members, friends, and acquaintances—not to mention myself—whose lives haven't gone exactly the way they had planned. They've suffered broken marriages, job difficulties, and anxieties, tortured for years by Satan each day.

We need to let go of our past, get up, dust ourselves off, and go again. There is not enough time to mope around and feel sorry for ourselves. We have work to do for Christ! What are you waiting for? Time is of the essence.

Philippians 3:13b-14 (KJV) says, "Forgetting those things which are behind and reaching forth unto those things that are before. I press toward the mark for the prize of the high calling of God in Christ Jesus." This scripture lets us know we cannot overcome without Jesus. It takes going through Jesus to get to God. And by doing this, he will give us the strength to overcome the negative things that Satan will try to make us think about ourselves. With God's forgiveness, we can forgive ourselves.

CHAPTER 15

ENCOURAGING YOURSELF BY CHANGING YOUR THOUGHT LIFE

I had been a little down. Because of this weakness in my body, I was facing an attack from Satan in my mind. I had to readjust my thinking so that I remembered the good things of God. I felt I needed to encourage myself by reading God's Word.

Philippians 4:8 (KJV) says, "Finally brethren, whatsoever things are true, whatsoever things are honest, whatsoever things are just, whatsoever things are pure, whatsoever things are lovely, whatsoever things are of good report; if there be any virtue, and if there be any praise, think on these things."

I then remembered seeing this same scripture marked in my mother's Bible. In the margin she had written that it was her favorite scripture. A smile came to my face, and a tear fell from my eye. I knew that God has a plan for all his children and that he doesn't want us to be discouraged or worried. He is always there, and to his Word, we can go to find whatever we may need. He will lift our spirits, and in him, we can be joyful and not waste our thoughts on Satan.

Just this one little nugget of hope through God's Word gave me strength for today. I knew that tomorrow would be tomorrow, and I knew that God would encourage me through his Word or the inspiration he often gave me through listening to and trusting the spirit inside of me.

I learned that Satan desires to sift us as wheat, but God is stronger than him. If we lean on God, he will bring his promises to pass. God doesn't want anyone to perish but to be hopeful, happy, and free. This is what we have to do. Encourage yourself during life's journey.

Luke 22:31–32a (KJV) says, "And the Lord said Simon, Simon, behold, Satan hath desired to sift you as wheat: but I have prayed for thee, that thy faith fail not."

What is your thought life? Ask yourself this question.

Romans 12:2 (KJV) says, "And be not conformed to this world: but be ye transformed by the renewing of your mind, that ye may prove what is that good and acceptable, perfect will of God."

Second Corinthians 10:4–5 (KJV) says,

> For the weapons of our warfare are not carnal, but mighty through God to the pulling down of strongholds. Casting down imaginations (wrong thoughts in your mind) and every high thing that exalts itself against the knowledge of God, bringing into captivity every thought to the obedience of Christ.

Chapter 16

Children Are Our Heritage

I pondered and prayed many times, asking God to save my children, grandchildren, and all my family and friends. I would also ask God to please save the world. At times I would feel so saddened about the end of this world and the ones who would not make heaven their home. I would seem to mourn even people I had not met because they were not saved.

I somehow had this deep revelation that through following Jesus (having a heart for God through Jesus Christ) and through praying for our heritage, our children and our children's children would be saved. I knew that God still answered the prayers of our mothers, fathers, grandparents, and great-grandparents.

I found in the scriptures that in the beginning God had a good plan. Genesis 1:27–28 (KJV) says, "This scripture is talking about how God made man in his own image and blessed them to be fruitful and to replenish and subdue the earth."

Acts 16:27–34 (KJV) says, "These scriptures speak of Paul and Silas being in prison, the angel of the Lord freed them. The keeper of the prison asked them what he needed to do to be saved. Paul told him to believe on the Lord Jesus Christ, and he shall be saved, he and his house."

Genesis 48:4, 8, 9 (KJV) says,

> In these scriptures Jacob said to Joseph that God had said unto him, "Behold, I will make thee fruitful, and multiply thee, and I will make of the multitude a people; and will give this land to thy seed after thee for an everlasting possession." And Israel (Jacob) beheld Joseph's sons and said, "Who are these?" And Joseph said unto his father, "They are my sons whom God hath given me in this place." And Jacob said, "Bring them, I pray thee, unto me, and I will bless them."

Isaiah 54:13 (KJV) says, "And all thy children shall be taught of the Lord; and great shall be the peace of thy children."

Isaiah 55:11–12b (KJV) says, "So shall my word be that goeth forth out of my mouth; it shall not return unto me void, but it shall accomplish that which I please, and it shall prosper in the thing whereto I sent it. For you shall go out with joy and be led forth with peace."

God's Word is true, and it will not return void.

Chapter 17

A Mother's Love

My mother was the best mom in the world. At least that's what I thought as a child, and I still do. Mama, as I called her, went to heaven more than two decades ago. Losing my mom was one of the hardest realities I had to face in my life, and I never got over it either. I just learned to live without her in my life.

With so many good memories of my mother, I understand now that she taught me how important it is to be a caring mother. She taught me about love, respect, being joyful, responsibility, honesty, and doing what's right. She trained all her children to serve the Lord, and she instilled in me the lesson that anything worth doing is worth doing right.

Being a mother or a father is a day-by-day walk. No one will ever get it exactly right, but God looks at our hearts. With his guidance, we can be vessels for him to use in order to train our children and raise them up by his Word.

Proverbs 22:6 (KJV) says, "Train up a child in the way he should go and when he is old he will not depart from it." I noticed this scripture says, "When he is old he will not depart." God's love and grace will safely keep him through life because of this training and the prayers he received as a child.

Being a good mom or dad is of the uttermost importance. Everyone has a calling. Parents mold the future of our world. Our contributions are very important to our society both in the present and in the future.

So be encouraged. God knew what he was doing when he gave you that child. By God's grace, you can accomplish the Father's will. We might not have all the gifts, and we might feel we are not gifted at all; however, God gives to us accordingly.

To those who do still have their mothers or dads in their lives, honor and cherish them. Show them every day that you love them, not just in words but in actions. Life is a short journey. You only have one time around. Make it your best circle, for soon you or people you love will pass on. Be nice, honest, and respectful of your mom and dad. Then you will have no regrets.

Chapter 18

Wisdom and Knowledge Obtained through Respect and Love for Others

We go through different phases of life. We are born as babies, and then we grow to small children, teens, adults, and then elderly people.

I watched people for years, studying the pattern of what was happening in their lives. Even children who had been trained from babies to do good sometimes grow up to rebel and disrespect authority, their parents, and their grandparents.

As a child, I thought hard about how some children, young adults, and even adults treated their parents and grandparents. I saw how they even treated elderly people in general with no respect.

When I was a child, my mother worked in a nursing home. I saw and felt the tears of these elderly people who never had visitors. It touched my heart. At the age of sixteen, I worked in a retail store, and one time I noticed a small child cursing her grandmother. This grandmother seemed so hurt, and she clearly didn't know how to handle the situation in public. In my lifetime I have seen so much disrespect from children, young adults, and other adults. Sometimes they don't call their elders or even check on them on a regular basis.

I've known a few elderly parents who haven't seen their adult children for ten to twenty years. They often say their grown children are just too busy and don't have the time. This is a growing problem in our society, and we need to put it to an end. It's all just a lack of love.

Matthew 24:12 (KJV) says, "Because iniquity shall abound, the love of many shall wax cold." This shouldn't be! God is not pleased with this behavior. Many elderly are alone with no way to go anywhere. They receive no phone calls, and no one in this life seems to care. Their hearts are dying for touch, for affection. Some of these elderly people are full of insight and wisdom. They are mentors who are left alone, knowledge wasted. Many times I've seen young people congregate and never talk with the older person in the room. No one makes conversation with the older person. He or she is ignored. These young people think that the old person is dumb or behind the times. But wisdom we can learn from these potential mentors is unlimited and priceless.

I pray the love of God captures our babies, children, young adults, and older adults, filling them with love, wisdom, and the knowledge that can be obtained through the respect and love for all.

CHAPTER 19

THE CARNAL MIND-SET

Some might think that if they pay their tithes and go to church, they are really doing God's work. It doesn't work this way! Yes, it's good to pay your tithes. You should, but there is much more to it. It's about sowing mercy, about concern, about passion for others, about putting ourselves last and others first. In summation, we should pursue God's way or no way at all.

One of our main goals in going to church may be to find Christian friends, which is very important. But our main goal for going to church should be to worship God, giving and encouraging, seeking out new souls for Jesus Christ, and loving our neighbors as ourselves.

Romans 8:6–11 (KJV) says,

> For to be carnally minded is death, but to be spiritually minded is life and peace. Because the carnal mind is enmity against God; for it is not subject to the law of God, nor indeed can be. So then, those who are in the flesh cannot please God. But you are not in the flesh but in the Spirit, if indeed the Spirit of God dwells in you. Now if anyone does not have the Spirit of Christ, he is not His. And if Christ is in you, the body is dead because of sin, but the Spirit is life because of righteousness. But if the Spirit of Him who raised Jesus from the dead dwells in you, He

who raised Christ from the dead will also give life to your
mortal bodies through his Spirit who dwells in you.

This scripture should give us the encouragement to look forward and keep our hearts and mind on Jesus, for we all have things to accomplish for Christ.

Second Corinthians 5:20 (NKJV) says, "We are ambassadors for Christ, as though God were pleading through us: We implore in Christ's stead, be you reconciled to God."

CHAPTER 20

LIFE'S MIRACLES
YOUR MIRACLE OR NARROW ESCAPE

I thought about the many narrow escapes that my family and I had experienced just as I'm sure you and your family have had. I also thought about how God had taken care of my loved ones and me. Maybe this chapter will bring back your memories of the miracles that have taken place in your life.

At the age of five, I remember falling in the pond not far from our house. Two of my sisters just happened to see me fall in, and together, they pulled me out. I've always thought of this as one of the many miracles in my life. At the age of seven, I stepped up in a chair to help Mama stir the gravy. When I tilted the chair over, extremely hot gravy spilled onto one side of my face. I remember Mama hoping and praying my face would not be scarred. Today you can barely tell where I was burned. At age nineteen, married and expecting our first child, I was in a car wreck, totaling the car. My clothes were torn from my body, and glass peppered my hair. It was a miracle that I was okay. The ambulance driver rushed me to the hospital. I was crying and praying aloud, hoping my baby was okay. Two months later my beautiful daughter was born with no complications. We named her Penny.

God knew she would be okay. He had a purpose for her life. At two months old, she developed pneumonia. By the hand of doctors, God kept her alive. At the age of six, she was walking across the road after getting off the school bus, and an older man who was driving did not stop. The bus driver thought she had been hit by the car, but she had hurriedly walked back to the bus. I knew this was not a sudden decision but the hand of God. A few years later, our church group was at the lake. A young man from our church found her facedown in the water, but he managed to revive her. She told us later she remembered looking down from above when he was reviving her. I knew her spirit had left her body. Many times she had been rescued from death. Because of God's saving grace, Penny is still with us. For this I am eternally grateful. Today Penny and her husband have two beautiful daughters who love the Lord. God knew they would be born. We all have a purpose for God.

Sherry, my youngest daughter, has faced many health problems during her life. As a baby and into her teenage years, she was taken to many skin specialists. We have continually prayed for her healing. I know God hears our prayers, even though we might not get our breakthrough. I know God has designed a purpose for this suffering. As an adult, she still has this skin condition, which has caused arthritis in her joints, but she has become a very strong person because of her hardships and health problems. I thank God for her every day. As a baby, a toddler, a little girl, a teenager, and now an adult, she has helped me through so many down days. She and her husband have also been blessed with three beautiful daughters who love the Lord. I'm blessed with grandchildren and their families. God's free gift of love, mercy and grace made this possible.

If you are a mother, father, sister, brother, aunt, or uncle, I'm sure that you can relate to the joy that family brings. God is a good God who always hears our prayers, but he may not always answer our prayers the way we want him to. May God's divine will be done.

All families are here for a reason. We all need to seek God for that reason. God wants to work in all of us so that we don't live in vain.

I have learned to look at the little things God has done and to be thankful. God just wants us to love him, trust in him, and be at peace in our hearts even when the clouds rage.

Once again, we must realize that God's grace not only saves our souls but also keeps us safe through life's narrow escapes. Through his grace, he works miracles in all our lives.

Sometimes it's good to keep a journal of our daily interactions. Rereading it will remind us just how much God helps us and our loved ones while we continue on this journey called life.

CHAPTER 21

THANKFUL FOR SMALL THINGS
KNOWING THAT GOD IS OUR SOURCE

I have worked as a property manager for more than twenty years, and I often ask myself, "What am I doing in this profession?" I was reminded of a strange event that happened years ago when I was an assistant for a chiropractor. I had been hoping and praying for a better-paying job. I had been looking for an apartment to rent until my house was built. As I was driving into the entrance of this beautiful rental property, I heard a voice whisper in my ear, "One day you will be the manager of this property." I did rent an apartment there that day. A few months passed. I was very down and decided to call my pastor and his wife. I was still working at the chiropractor's office and had not gotten any kind of raise.

I asked my pastor and his wife to pray with me that I would get a better job. A few weeks passed. I went in to pay my rent and accidentally overheard the leasing consultant talking with someone on the phone, telling the person that this was her last day. She had given notice, and the property needed a leasing consultant. I filled out an application that day, got the job the next week, and was the property manager in seven months. Then, I remembered back to when I had heard those words whispered in my ear. I knew this had to be words from God. These words had come to pass. During my career as the manager at this property, it was never easy, but I kept my integrity and struggled to succeed, trying to remember the little things.

For example, one time when I was so busy that I didn't have time to go to lunch even though I was really hungry, one of my residents happened by and left me a small bowl of food. One time when I was decorating for Christmas, I spent all our budget on decorations. I put together a small Christmas flower arrangement for my assistant's desk, but I had none left for mine. I had a very small Christmas tree in the back of my truck but no decorations. I thought, *If I only had some small decorations, I could put this tree on my desk.* Then a resident walked in with a Christmas gift for me. She had bought me a box of tiny decorations. She had no idea I had this small tree. I knew this was God's way of blessing my efforts. As I travel back down memory lane, I remember when the elderly groundsman brought me roses, not knowing how I loved them, but God knew.

I feel all these little moments and blessings through life are God's way of encouraging us and reminding us about our relationship with him. He is a God to worship and praise, not only for the big things but for the small as well. God is our source.

Chapter 22

That's Just Life

Life happens. Some reach their goals, and others don't. I've included some stories here. (I have changed the names of the following friends and acquaintances I've met in life.)

Will was a very good young man, an overall great person. His wife and child were so very important to him. He was always so optimistic, so confident and happy with so much hope for his child to become very active in the church. He was always moving from church to church because he wanted his child to become a big part of the church in general. His child is now grown, and he has since moved away. His dream and hope never came true. I don't see him very often, but when I do, you can tell he is down and depressed because of his disappointments in life.

Sometimes our dreams and hopes do not align with what God dreams and hopes for our lives. That's just life, but God doesn't love us any less. When we are called home to God, no one will take anything with them. All belongs to God. He's all we have. He will guide you safely like no one else. Be happy, and rest in him. Be overcomers by the blood of Jesus Christ.

You might not reach your goal, but dig deeper in God, for he loves you more than you'll ever know. God always knows what is best for us.

What has God called us to do?

If you are called to do something small, it's still large in God's eyes. If you are called to do something large, it's no larger than the small thing your neighbor is doing. Serving God from our heart is what God wants, and consequently, God is so pleased with us because he sees he has our hearts.

In reading this book, I know you have learned, as I have, that there is no big or small acts in God's eyes. Ecclesiastes 9:10 (KJV) says, "Whatsoever your hand finds to do, do it with your might."

CHAPTER 23

SECOND-GUESSING GOD
LEARNING FROM LIFE'S JOURNEY

You might ask, "What is second-guessing God?" As we all know, people sometime try to figure out the answer God is going to give as we all pray to him about issues in our lives. God's Word says to be patient, and most of the time, we all run out of patience.

First Timothy 6:11b (NKJV), "Pursue righteousness, Godliness, faith, love, patience and gentleness."

There was a person—I'll call her Lynn—who had lost a well-paying job, but not because of anything she had done wrong. It was just a bad economy at the time. She had great credit, and she always paid her bills on time, tithed, gave donations, and volunteered places. She was such a light to others in her home community. With a need for a job, the church group would come together and pray daily for her to get back to work and bring home a weekly paycheck. She never gave up faith, although each time she was interviewed, the employers always hired someone else.

After six months of not knowing, family and friends figured there had to be doubt somewhere. Maybe Lynn did not believe in God's power. Family and friends began to second-guess God. They would often say that a good job should have come along by now. Her husband lost all faith, saying, "God must not care!" If he cared, her desire for a job would be fulfilled by now.

After a year of spending all their savings just trying to stay afloat, a call from an acquaintance came in. There was at last an opening for a job, and it was just in time! The paychecks started again, and things got back to normal. Lynn said this had been the longest year she had ever lived. Later Lynn told me many things that she had learned from that year of hardship. She now has the job of her dreams. The desire of her heart came to pass. With patience, she had waited for the position. I asked her, "What if you had not found a job? What if you had lost your home, land, and all you had?"

Lynn replied, "Oh, in my heart I gave up all those possessions a long time ago. I learned it's not things that keep us going but our faith in God, and our faith in God means trusting God in every circumstance we face. God is the only one who knows how much strength each one of us has." Lynn went on to say, "My God owns the cattle of a thousand hills. I alone have placed my heart and my life in his hands. I'm just along for the ride to my eternal home."

I went away that day, rejoicing over how much she had learned about God and her belief in God. Sometimes we have to look and observe what's going in other people's lives to get closer to God in our walk of faith. Sometimes we second-guess God, missing the whole point! We should not analyze the situation from a carnal mind.

Several years passed. I had worked as a property manager for almost fifteen years. The economy had gotten bad. Layoffs were happening everywhere. After getting to work, I received a phone call from my employer. I was let go because of the dragging economy. I had the highest salary there, and he could not pay me anymore. At first, I didn't feel anything. Then what exactly had happened sunk in. With the way the economy had gotten, no one knew who would be laid off next. Taking a deep breath, I looked at the positive. My employer had given me a letter of recommendation, but even after several months of trying, I still had no job, although my family and I had been praying and hoping a job would come along. I then remembered what had happened to Lynn. I made a point of trying to learn from what was happening. When I had taken this management job,

I had been praying and had heard a whisper in my ear. Or maybe it was a thought coming to my mind. Either way, I knew that this job was going to get me where I needed to be. At last, I felt the peace to keep going and believing. Months passed. I had learned much from this layoff. I knew now I had been putting my job first in my life. When I was managing the property, I hardly ever took lunch—unless I needed to run errands for my employer. Over the years I had actually given my whole life to my job. I also remembered how I had quit the worship team at my church because I felt like I needed to focus on my job. I remembered saying, "I can't do it all, so I'll just quit everything so that I will have a focus."

Looking back, I made my job my source, even though God was supposed to be my source. Once again, I had taken things into my own hands, planning it all out for myself.

Each day is a learning process. We must never think we have learned it all. We'll all be learning until we die if we are open to learning and trust God for his guidance. We are all on a journey. This journey is a gift from God, and through his grace we can make it successfully through our trials in life. Don't forget this. With God's love and grace, we cannot lose.

CHAPTER 24

JUDGE NOT THAT YOU BE NOT JUDGED
SELF-RIGHTEOUSNESS IS NOT LOVE

Years ago a friend of mine from high school—we'll call her Jean—told me a story I will always remember. It was a true story about what had happened to her because she was so quick to judge her classmates, teachers, and other acquaintances.

She told me about a beautiful classmate who was very well dressed—we'll call her Bee. This classmate seemed to have no friends. Rumor had it that she was stuck-up and that she thought she was better than everyone else. Jean went on to say that after three months of sitting next to Bee in the classroom, she decided to find out for herself who this girl really was. She just knew she was a spoiled brat, but she befriended her anyway simply because of her curiosity. With hesitation, she went up to her and talked about the weather, about their studies, and about anything she could think of. Jean rambled on and on. Bee just looked at her and began to cry. Bee thanked Jean for befriending her and said that she really needed a friend and that she had to do lots of reading, studying, and listening to keep up her studies. She really had no time for anything else. Bee went on to say that she and her mom lived alone. She explained how her mom worked two jobs to give her such nice clothes. Jean felt Bee's sincerity. Bee said the reason she needed to keep making all As was because she wanted to go to college and help her mom someday. Bee talked for a while, sharing her good and bad times. Jean found out that Bee was the only child and was a little shy, so she didn't know how to approach people to make friends. At this point Jean felt so ashamed for judging her. They became best friends from that day forward.

Another story I remember came from a coworker of mine. He told me he didn't like pretty stuck-up blondes in school and that he never approached them. They were too sophisticated for him. He had been out of school for almost twenty years, and his cousin set him up on a blind date. At first, when he saw his date, a beautiful blonde, he wanted to run away, but he and his cousin were already in front of her house when out she walked. He said he wanted to push the accelerator and leave, but out of respect, he stayed. He said he always judged by outward appearances, but he found out quickly he had been wrong all along. She wasn't that mean blonde that he had judged her to be. He said she was the nicest, sweetest girl he had ever met. She was just the kind of girl he had been looking for. Today they are happily married with two great kids.

Matthew 7:1–3 (KJV) says, "Judge not that you be not judged. For with what judgment you judge, you will be judged: and with the measure you use, it will be measured back to you. And why do you look at the speck in your brother's eye, but do not consider the plank in your own eye."

One of my female friends came to me years ago after she had bumped into an old classmate in the grocery aisle. She had known this lady all her life, but she had not seen her in years. My friend went on to say, "I was so happy to see her, but there was a self-righteousness about her, a 'better than you' approach. I was simply crushed. My heart was broken. She looked righteous on the outside, but I felt no love, no concern. It was as if she had never known me. The last time I saw her, we attended the same church. All was well, but we took different roads with our lives. Now we aren't of the same denomination, but I am a Christian. I knew she was judging me, but she didn't know anything about me." Then my friend asked me, "How can you love God and not love your neighbor?"

I knew this was scripture and began thinking, *I know we should love one another and not be so quick to judge.* I went home that day and prayed for God to change the ungodly ways we as humans sometime take on when we look at the other person. After all, God is the only one who knows their heart.

Romans 13:9b–10 (NKJV) says, "You shall love your neighbor as yourself. Love does no harm to his neighbor; therefore, love is the fulfillment of the law."

I believe God looks on self-righteousness as the utmost evil. It's a deception, a way that seems right but isn't. Self-righteousness is a form of religion. God doesn't want religion! We should ask ourselves, "Am I self-righteous, or is my heart full of love and concern for the lost, the weak, and the afraid?"

Proverbs 14:12 (NKJV) says, "There is a way that seems right unto a man, but the end thereof are the ways of death." We would not know God and this love he has bestowed upon each of us if it were not for his grace. This is the message we should learn—love. Love is fulfilling the law of grace as it was given to us when Jesus died on the cross for our sins.

Matthew 5:43–47 (NKJV) says,

> You have heard that it was said, You shall love your neighbor and hate your enemy. But I say to you, love your enemies, bless those who curse you, do good to those who hate you, and pray for those who spitefully use you and persecute you, that you may be the sons of your Father in heaven; for he makes his sun rise on the evil and on the good, and sends rain on the just and on the unjust. For if you love those who love you, what reward have you? And if you greet your brethren only, what do you do more than others?

As soon as I read this scripture, I remembered a dream I had of forgiving a few people who had wronged me. I had worked for them for a few years and had given them my best. In my dream I went to them and repeatedly told them I had forgiven them for the bad deeds they had done. I said,

"I forgive you. I forgive you. I forgive you." I made my voice louder with each sentence.

When I awoke from the dream, I knew God was saying to me that I had not forgiven completely. I needed to practice forgiving fully from the heart. I suddenly felt so much peace and serenity. It was such a good feeling of perfect surrender to God. I had given it all to God, not just from the mouth but from the heart.

CHAPTER 25

HELL IS NOT MADE FOR YOU
TIME FOR A HEART CHANGE

So many live in fear of hell, but hell was made for the devil and his angels. God did not make hell for us, but we will go there if we do not accept Christ in our hearts. God doesn't want us to go to hell, so he sent his Son, Jesus, to die for our sins.

Matthew 25:41b (KJV) says, "Jesus was speaking to the unsaved ones, 'Depart from me, you cursed into everlasting fire prepared for the devil and his angels.'" Notice that it says the devil and his angels. Yes, it's your choice. You choose.

Joshua 24:15 (KJV) says, "In Joshua's exhortation to Israel, he said, 'Choose you this day whom you will serve.' And Joshua went on to say, 'As for me and my house, we will serve the Lord.'"

Matthew 6:24 (NKJV) says, "Jesus said, 'No one can serve two masters; for either he will hate the one and love the other, or else he will be loyal to the one and despise the other. You cannot serve God and mammon (evil).'"

Proverbs 14:12 (KJV) says, "There is a way which seemeth right unto a man, but the end thereof are the ways of death."

To give this previous scripture some clarity: A man may persuade himself that his sin, his evil dealings, his false religion, and his selfish ways are right, but whatever is not God's way will end in death and hell. So you see, once again, it's all about a heart change.

First Samuel 16:7b (KJV) says, "For man looks on the outward appearance, but the Lord looks on the heart."

I remember my granddaughter Kayla (age eleven) saying, "Nona, God looks at our heart. It doesn't matter what we look like." Wisdom often came from this child. Isaiah 11:16 (KJV) says, "And a little child shall lead them."

We cannot change ourselves. We have to fully depend on God. This means asking for his forgiveness, inviting him into our heart, and relying completely on him through his Son, Jesus Christ, for the heart change we need and for the life we should live.

CHAPTER 26

A BETTER LIFE
LIVING AND LEARNING

Psalm 118:24 (KJV) says, "This is the day that the Lord hath made, I will rejoice and be glad in it." Live life to the max. Don't let Satan steal from you. These promises are yours to keep, freely given to you by God.

In writing this book and listening to what God had to say, I came to realize that every moment I didn't live life as God would have me, I was letting Satan steal these moments from me. We don't have to accept Satan's art of craftiness, but we can draw from the well of God's grace, love, and forgiveness, giving our lives fully to God.

I remember a Christian lady apologizing to me that she was not going to attend the Sunday morning service because of her friend's wedding. She kept making excuses. I knew at that point that Satan was condemning her. I said to her, "You are a child of God wherever you are. There you have your cause."

Her eyes widened, and she replied, "Thank you for that." I knew she suddenly realized that she had been feeling condemned and that she could be used by God anywhere and everywhere. God's peace, love, and guidance were all with her.

Philippians 4:7 (NKJV) says, "And the peace of God, which surpasses all understanding, will guard your hearts and minds through Christ Jesus."

Hebrews 13:20–21 (KJV) says, "The God of peace make you complete in every good work to do his will, working in you what is well pleasing in his sight, through Jesus Christ."

Once again, I had learned how to lead this better life through Jesus and none other by accepting his love and grace.

CHAPTER 27

ABSTAINING FROM EVIL

First Thessalonians 5:22 (KJV) says, "Abstain from all appearance of evil." You might direct teens or anyone of any age by teaching them abstinence. The strength to abstain is just another one of God's gifts obtained only by his love and grace.

Abstinence: Abstinence means abstaining (staying away) from what would be a wrong choice for you. Abstinence is really something to be proud of. It's a gift from God. Today it takes a lot of strength to be abstinent from things such as running with the wrong crowd, sex before marriage, drinking, drugs, bullying, lying, hatred, envy, rebellion, cheating, stealing, cursing, laziness, procrastination, and overeating, just to name a few.

Teen pressure is a growing trend. Who can stop this? Teenagers can start today by making the right choices and doing the right thing. You can change society just by starting today.

Attitude: A person with a good attitude works well with others and is liked by many. Friends and others who don't know him or her watch this person. A good attitude gets you further in life than pouting and throwing temper tantrums. Things seem to work out better with a positive attitude.

Blessing: God has blessed us as a nation. God's blessings will be on us if we continue to keep the outlook we need. We in America are a blessed people, and we should be thankful of who we are and the talents, opportunities, and freedom we have.

Strength: God will give us the strength we need to rise above adversity.

Temptation: Resist temptation. You might ask, "How do I do this?" It is much easier to focus on what you want your destination to be if you love yourself and remember that we are wonderfully made by God. Don't get sidetracked along the way. Try to focus on your goal and walk forward each day.

Integrity: Be true to yourself, serving Christ and walking with honor, honesty, humbleness, and love. This is who God has called you to be. Sharing the life you live could help others more than you'll ever know. Remember, someone is always watching. If you lose your integrity, you might get it back, but it could take others a long time to trust you again, so make sure you maintain this gift of integrity God has given you. You might just help many find their way.

Nature: The nature of a good man or woman. Putting on the Nature of Christ. With this, you can surmount the spiritual mountains in life. With God's protection, you can be the ambassador God has called you to be. You'll be on a mission for Christ with his covering.

Endurance: You must endure as a good soldier of Christ. God will give you the strength to endure as you walk toward your goal to please our Savior and Lord. He provides us with the food or other substance necessary for growth, health, and good condition.

Nourish: To nourish is to cherish, nurture, foster, harbor, nurse, entertain, maintain, sustain, provide, keep, hold, and have. The Lord has us safely protected in his arms. John 10:28–30 (KJV) says, "I give unto them eternal life; and they shall never perish, Neither shall any man pluck them out of my Father's hand."

Compromise: Do not compromise. You might have many so-called friends, acquaintances, and even kindred spirits who may want you to compromise. They might ask things of you that you know are wrong or that do not agree with the Christian guidelines in your Bible. Just remember to follow your heart. Wrong choices have consequences. Most of the time, these wrong choices end up in failure. You may have to walk a long, hard road back to the right one.

Enjoyment: Enjoy your life with the fruits of the Spirit, which will make your life much easier. Galatians 5:22–23 (KJV) says, "The fruit of the Spirit is love, joy, peace, longsuffering, gentleness, goodness, faith, meekness, temperance (self-control)."

Here is a scripture about the works of the flesh. Galatians 5:19–21 (KJV) says,

> Now the works of the flesh are manifest, which are these; Adultery, fornication, uncleanness, lasciviousness (showing lust), Idolatry (worshipping an idol, or loving something more than you love God), witchcraft (superstitions or powers of influence), hatred, variance (a disagreeing or a falling out, discord), emulations (desire to equal or excel, rivalry), wrath (very angry, rage), strife (quarreling, fighting), seditions (discontent or rebellion), heresies (disunified belief), envyings, murders, drunkenness, revellings (disorderly merry good time), and such like; they which do such things will not inherit the kingdom of God.

CHAPTER 28

YOUTH DISCOURAGEMENT

Our children and children's children, our friends' children, our relatives, our acquaintances, and all our young people need someone to guide them and teach them the way to Jesus Christ. You might not think they want your help and concern, but in their hearts they do. This is a hard world to live in, and it is our responsibility to bridge the gap. Each day we should pray for all. Everyone is important. Every soul needs to surrender to Christ, and through our lives and our prayers, hearts can be changed. This is a much-needed encouragement.

As a teenager, my granddaughter Lakan talked to her teachers at her school and asked if she and a friend could put out posters inviting classmates to take part in an abstinence program that they were trying to begin. Not many were interested, so the program ended before it began. I felt her discouragement and prayed she would be okay.

We never know what roads we will face in life, but one thing I know for sure is that God is in control. He knows our end from our beginning.

Whatever we are facing, there is an answer. He has a path he wants us to take. Sometimes we are knocked down like Lakan was, but we must get up, keep going, and keep believing that God has a plan for our lives. God's grace is sufficient.

So here we have it again. God does care for all.

Chapter 29

The Gifts of God's Grace in a Bundle
A God of Love

I was awakened in the night, thinking of all God's gifts of grace. A list of verbs, adverbs, and adjectives came to mind. There were so many— laughter, smiling, giving, loving, admiring, encouraging, helping, befriending, kindness, boldness, gentleness, exhortation, forgiving, accepting, comforting, sharing, among others.

Sometimes God helps and heals us through one another. What gift is yours? How do we fit? It's time to pick up our cross, follow Christ, and obey his calling. We can make such a big difference in someone else's life just by being obedient.

Isaiah 1:19 (KJV) says, "If you be willing and obedient, you shall eat the good of the land." Now join me in the following prayer and give your life to Christ:

> First, admit you are a sinner. Second, be willing to turn from sin (repent). Third, believe that Jesus Christ died for you, was buried, and rose from the dead. Fourth, invite Jesus Christ into your heart to be your personal Savior.

> Read and study your Bible daily to know Christ better. Talk to God in prayer each day. Communication with the Lord lets him know you are his and that you are

committed to him. Trust and have faith in Jesus Christ, the Lord of your life.

Get baptized, worship, and fellowship with Christians in a Bible-based church.

Tell others about Christ.

CHAPTER 30

WHAT'S LEFT?

I realized I was getting closer to my senior years. I asked myself these questions: "What in life have I accomplished for God? What good have I done? Have I grown spiritually?" At that point, God's Spirit within me gave me the answers.

My frustration turned into peace. My thoughts were of life, not death. My depression was now joy. My thoughts were ones of happiness. I accepted the fact that I was in God and he was in me.

I knew that the rest of my life would be even better because I had grown to know that he is who he says he is and that he really does love everyone. Our lives are complete in him, and this is the only way we can be fully complete.

First John 4:8 (KJV) says, "For God is love." Second Corinthians 12:9 (KJV) says, "God's grace is sufficient for all."

CHAPTER 31

WORDS OF ENCOURAGEMENT

There are so many scriptures of encouragement all over the Bible. Here are a few.

Isaiah 41:10 (KJV) says, "Do not fear, I am with you. I will strengthen and uphold you with my righteous hand."

John 14:27 (KJV) says, "Peace I leave with you, my peace I give you. Do not let your hearts be troubled and do not be afraid."

Proverbs 18:10 (KJV) says, "The name of the Lord is a fortified tower, the righteous run into it and are safe."

Psalms 120:1 (KJV) says, "I call on the Lord in my distress and he hears me."

First Peter 5:7 (KJV) says, "Casting all your care upon him; for he careth for you."

The Lord wants us to be encouraged. Satan is the accuser of the brethren and wants to fill us with anxiety and frustration. Satan tries to take away our peace, but God is our strong tower for all the days of our lives. You've heard the saying "Let go and let God." This is what God is trying to say to us through the scriptures. Rest in him.

Matthew 11:28–29 (KJV) says, "Come unto me all who labor and are heavy laden, and I will give you rest. Take my yoke upon you and learn of me, for I am meek and lowly in heart, and you will find rest for your souls; For my yoke is easy and my burden is light."

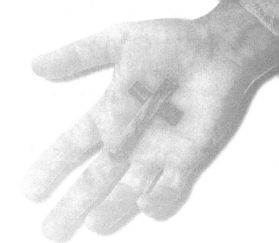

CHAPTER 32

PERFECTION

I was brought up in a very strict legalistic church, and I thought we were supposed to be perfect, which is impossible, for only God is perfect.

I know now that no human has ever been perfect except Jesus, and he was God in the flesh. And how did I learn this? I learned this lesson from my seven-year-old granddaughter Kaitlin. I had been working on a project and trying to get it perfect when she said, "Nona, nothing is perfect."

No, nothing is perfect, is it? Only Jesus Christ is perfect. Second Corinthians 5:21 (KJV) says, "For he hath made him to be sin for us, who knew no sin; that we might be made the righteousness of God in him."

As I was taught from childhood in this church, one had to reach perfection. Boy, how I tried! I didn't want anything to jeopardize my chances of going to heaven. Well, being good is one thing, but being fanatic and so fearful is another.

I learned that we should do our best, always remembering that we will never be perfect. Our perfection rests in God's Son, Jesus.

Jesus dying on the cross for our sins was enough. God only wants the human race to have a perfect heart toward him.

John 3:16 (KJV) says, "For God so loved the world, he gave his only begotten son, that whosoever believeth in him should not perish but have everlasting life."

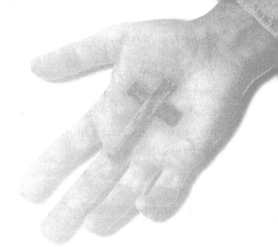

CHAPTER 33

GOD IS REAL

God is *real*. Why should we think this? The Word of God is true. If you follow scripture, everything comes to pass just like it is written.

We live in perilous times. Second Timothy 3:1 (KJV) says, "This also know, that in the last days perilous days shall come." Matthew 24:6 (KJV) speaks of wars and rumors of wars.

Mark 13:8 (KJV) says, "Nation shall rise up against nation and kingdom against kingdom. There shall be earthquakes in divers places, and there shall be famines and troubles. These are the beginning of sorrows."

Yes, the Bible is proven to be true from the beginning of time.

I know that God is real because he lives in my heart. I could not get through one day without him. He has answered prayers that I have prayed. He is my all, my hope, my strength, my everything, and I will serve only him.

Hebrews 9:14 (KJV) says, "How much more shall the blood of Jesus Christ, who through the eternal spirit offered himself without spot to God, purge your conscience from dead works to serve the living God."

Ephesians 3:16 (KJV) says, "That he would grant you, according to the riches of his glory, to be strengthened with might by his spirit in the inner man."

We can have faith and know by the scriptures that God is real. Any strength we have comes from within our hearts if we accept Christ as the Lord of our lives. With this acceptance that God is real, we have peace that passes understanding within our hearts. This inner peace proves to us that God is real.

Philippians 4:7 (KJV) says, "The peace of God which passes all understanding, shall keep your hearts and minds through Christ Jesus."

CHAPTER 34

MAKING RIGHT CHOICES GIVEN TO US BY GOD'S GRACE

Sometimes making right choices is not easy, especially for teenagers who are already under so much peer pressure, but in the long run, it sure makes life's journey a lot less complicated if you make the right choices. Choose what's right. Don't run with the wrong crowd. Refrain from lying, cheating, stealing, cursing, rioting, doing drugs, drinking, and other disruptive actions. Be respectful to one another. Keep the laws of the land. You'll find that doing so will make for a much better life.

No, life will never be perfect. There will always be hard bumps in the road, but it's what we do with what we are given and our outlook on things that determines how happy and peaceful we are.

Making decisions can sometimes be difficult. Through life's journey one might be confused about what the right decision is. What right decision is best for you, your child, or your spouse? It's good to weigh the pros and cons. Write down the advantages and disadvantages of a situation with a paper and pen, and then decide what is the best decision at the time. We all do this, don't we? Yes, we should evaluate and not rush into making decisions—who to marry, who to date, what job to take, what house to buy, what car to purchase, what bank to use, what church to attend, even how many children to have. The list goes on and on. Life is full of decisions and choices. Let us make the right ones.

One person cannot decide for another what the right decision is. Only you can decide what is best for your life. Only you can make that right choice. Wrong choosing lead to painful outcomes, such as physical and mental stress, financial difficulties, divorce, loneliness, and much worse.

Cheryl (age sixteen) felt peer pressure. In Sunday school she often told stories about her life. She was an avid reader, reading her Bible daily and always depending on the Bible for instruction about making the right choices and decisions in her life. She said her Bible gave her direction, foundation, and strong ethics (moral standards). She spoke of her respect and admiration for her parents too. She had a very close relationship with them, and this was definitely a plus.

Listed here are a few of Cheryl's favorite scriptures from her Bible:

Ephesians 6:1–2 says, "Children obey your parents in the Lord for this is right. Honor thy Father and Mother which is the first commandment with promise."

Ephesians 6:7–8 says, "With good will, doing service to the Lord and not to men. Knowing that what good thing you do you will receive of the Lord."

Ephesians 6:11 says, "Put on the whole armor of God that you may be able to stand against the wiles of the devil."

Ephesians 6:14–18 says,

> Stand, having your loins girt about with truth and having on the breastplate of righteousness and your feet shod with the preparation of the gospel of peace. Above all, taking the shield of faith wherewith you shall be able to quench all the fiery darts of the wicked. And take the helmet of salvation and the sword of the Spirit which is the Word of God. Praying always with all prayer and all supplication in the Spirit and watching with all perseverance (steady and continued action) and supplication (humble and sincere appeal) for all saints.

CHAPTER 35

PARENTING
MAINTAINING A BALANCE WITH
THE HELP OF JESUS CHRIST

We should value parenting with balance. After all, we are teaching and molding children, America's future adults, into the persons they need to be, people who are full of integrity and kindness, possessing strong principles and leadership abilities, steadfastly adhering to high moral standards.

But what is this *balance*? These young people must receive a healthy balance of *love* and *discipline*. This healthy balance will give these future men and women a steady foundation and instill in them self-worth and respect not only for themselves but for others too.

You might think you love your children by never saying no to them, by working two jobs to give them everything they want, and by giving them allowances based on chores they complete. You never argue because you hate the drama. You don't want to upset your children, so you just let things slide. You procrastinate, thinking you'll talk to them about their behavior later.

Now not all parents think this way, but believe it or not, some parents are missing the discipline part. The world knows you love your child, but sometimes love takes being stern, being blunt, and saying no. So many parents are trying to be their children's friends instead of their disciplinarians. Parents need to take the love they have for their children and mix it with positive discipline and guidance.

So many parents didn't have this blend of love and discipline as children. Because they were not taught good behavior, some are raising children without knowing how, ruling with harsh discipline (with no love) or either love (with no discipline).

Our society, parents, and teachers need to affirm and support studies as part of the curriculum of our schools and churches. There are many programs that we can use as tools, teaching these kids (our future) how to be better men and women.

As parents, we will have much better success with disciplining our children if we follow Christ and accept his gift of love and guidance, for he loves us so much and is always there for us as a leader when we don't know where to turn. If we reach out to him, we can make it through these years of parenting.

There are so many gifts Christ gives us. He teaches us how to be parents. Loving our child is a gift from God. The ability to be patient but bold is yet another gift.

Above all, life in general is such a sweet gift from the Father above. God is good, and through following Jesus Christ, we can maintain a healthy balance of parenting (preparing our children to be the adults God wants them to be.)

CHAPTER 36

CHERISH THE MOMENT
ALL MOMENTS ARE GIFTS FROM GOD

Live life to the fullest. Cherish the moment. After all, this moment could be your last in this life. Enjoy those grandchildren. Take pleasure in those strolls in the park. Take a picture of the blue sky. Capture the fragrance, the color of the flowers, and the trees that surround you. Be young at heart, not an old grouch. Have fun, joke around, clown around, and dance. Be thankful for small things, for these matter the most in life. Sing while doing laundry. Run and play with your pets. Be optimistic about life. Eat dessert. Just don't overdo it. Dream big, and love big.

As humans, we have no power over the grave. Faith works. Faith in Jesus Christ as our Savior will keep us safe. There is a time for all things. Ecclesiastes 3:2–3 (KJV) says, "A time to be born, a time to die, a time to heal, a time to plant." And the scripture goes on.

Jane, a great girl with much optimism, had a T-shirt made just for herself. It read, "Cherish the Moment." Under the wording was a large smiley face. Jane passed away a few years back, but everyone she knew remembered the red tee she designed for herself with that smiley face on the front. Yes, she was a girl with a smile. Jane enjoyed each moment she lived. Whenever I thought of Jane, my granddaughter Ana would came to mind.

Ana always wears a smile, even when I know she feels discouraged. She has never complained to me. The world would be a better place to live in if we all could smile more. Give it all to God, and let his grace work in us.

Let's make a point to cherish the moment. This will not only make our lives better but also rejuvenate other people's lives through our happiness and love. This love and happiness are gifts received from Jesus Christ, the *hope* of our calling.

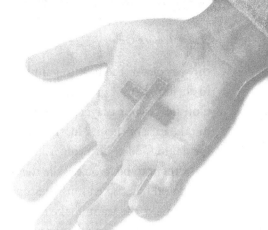

CHAPTER 37

MEDIOCRE
BY GOD, YOU ARE WONDERFULLY MADE

In *Webster's Dictionary*, mediocre means "ordinary; neither good or bad; barely adequate."

Have you ever felt that you were *mediocre*? Most of us are mediocre. You are cute but not beautiful. You have a great personality but not the best. You're good at singing, playing sports, whistling, riding a bike, driving a car, cooking, sewing, and so on but just not the best. You're just kind of good at anything you do. I've heard it said, "You're a jack-of-all-trades and a master of none." Most school-age kids today think they are *mediocre,* and they probably are; however, being *mediocre can be a good thing.* With all the talent and training opportunities available today, even *mediocre* kids can become what they want to be if their parents can afford it. But what about the children of parents who live from paycheck to paycheck and can't afford it? *Most of us fit in this category.* These mediocre kids are left out unless they have an overwhelming faith and trust in God that they are wonderfully made. It takes extra boldness and lots of stamina for these kids to stand out and take a lead in sports, school activities, or any other achievement.

What can we do? We can start teaching our children when they are born, giving them confidence in themselves by the way we treat and respect them. Above all things, pray for them, but let them learn from their mistakes the way you did. As they grow into adults, children have to be thrown out of the nest to gain this confidence. You love them and want to shelter them, but sheltering is sometimes bad when it's time to let go. God hears your prayers, and you must give them to God and trust him to take care of them. No, they might not be perfect children, but they are special to God and to you. You want them to be themselves, not what *you* want them to be. Don't make them take piano lessons because *you* wished you could have taken music lessons, make them play ball just because *you* didn't make the team, make them run a marathon because it's *your* desire, make straight As in school and college so that *you* can brag about them getting better grades than the other students, make them wear their hair the way *you* want it, or make them walk or sit the way *you* want them to. God made us all. We are wonderfully made. We are gifts of God's grace.

Psalm 139:14 (KJV) says, "I will praise thee; for I am fearfully and wonderfully made: marvellous are thy works; and that my soul knoweth right well."

God made you to be you and to be his servant. Don't worry about not being the best. If you are you and have asked Jesus into your heart, then you are the best you there is.

God has a plan for your life. Seek his plan. Romans 12:2 (KJV) says, "Be not conformed to this world, but be transformed by the renewing of your mind, that you may prove what is that good, acceptable and perfect will of God."

CHAPTER 38

LOVE
A FEELING OF HEART CRY

Some say that love is the best feeling in the world. Part of the lyrics to the song "The Rose," which is so beautifully sung by Bette Midler, included, "Just remember in the winter far beneath the bitter snow lies the seed that with the sun's love in the spring becomes the rose." And remember the old saying "Love is a feeling that you feel when you feel you have a feeling that you've never felt before." Most everyone has heard this quote, possibly from their parents, grandparents, teachers, or friends.

Sometimes people are missing the love they need in their lives. Sometimes the heart cries so deep that there is no tears to shed. You might ask, "What does love have to do with a heart crying?" There are lots of hurting people out there. People may smile, but in the deepness of their hearts, they are crying for someone to love them, someone to reach out, someone like a parent, a sibling, a friend, or maybe even a spouse. You'd be surprised. Some even share the same home. Here's a story that will make your heart cry.

Leah knew this feeling of her heart crying. She grew up in an orphanage, and she was a really good Christian lady. She was loved, but she never had the love of her own mom and dad. At age eighteen she fell in love and married her first love, John. They moved miles away to a small community. Only a few days after their wedding, John developed pneumonia and passed away. Leah felt alone. Her heart cried.

A few days after John's funeral, Leah began going all through the neighborhood to make friends since she was new to the community, but only one neighbor, a little old lady who lived at the end of her street, befriended her. Leah baked cookies and rang doorbells every day, and not one person from the neighborhood invited her over. One day as she was raking leaves, she waved at the neighbors passing by, but no one showed any friendliness. Days passed. Months passed. Leah felt alone, and her heart cried endlessly. Then one day the little old lady at the end of her street invited her to visit the small country church just up the road. The members of the little church showed that they cared. Leah's heart crying was healed through their love.

Leah had been thinking about going back to the orphanage for a visit since it was the only real home she had ever known. She had so many memories of the orphanage from her childhood. She was hoping things had not changed. Walking into the hallway of the orphanage, she met Mary, a little ten-year-old girl. Leah felt a real closeness for this little girl, so she decided to start the adoption process the very next week. Finally, with all the paperwork completed, Leah was so thrilled to bring Mary home, and Mary was so happy to have her own mom too. Most of the time, it was just the two of them. No one in their community ever visited them except a few from her church and the little old lady just up the street. The love Leah and Mary shared was so great.

Years passed. Mary finished high school and went onto college, which was hours away. Leah was alone again, and her heart was crying. Right after graduation Mary married and moved far away. Leah kissed her goodbye. Leah's heart cried once more. Leah had been a great mom to Mary, giving her love and security, but now it was time for Mary to make a home of her own.

What can we learn from this story?

First, life is short. Life is lived in stages, and each stage of life must come to an end. The love between a parent and a child is so important in both of their lives. So whether you have a little family or a large family, cherish it nonetheless.

Second, the reality is that some people are alone! It's not clear how or why this happens, but sometimes people get lost in the shuffle of other people's lives. Kids grow up and move away. Spouses die. Sometimes others are so busy with their own lives that there just isn't room for you. It just happens. But God will move someone else into your life if you let him, and this person is often called a friend.

Do you know someone whose life you can make better? The little old lady at the end of your street, a family member, a mom, a dad, an acquaintance, or someone who lives all alone? Can you give them a call, pay them a visit, or send them a text? Just saying, "I love you," would rid one of his or her heart cries.

What are some other points we can ponder?

- One act of kindness can change a life.

- Compassion from the heart can change a nation.

- Forgiveness brings peace.

- To love the unlovable is true love.

- We should give to others each day as servants.

- Helping a friend is unselfishness.

- Just being there for others can make a difference.

- One ounce of love is of great value, but one ounce of hatred is sin.

All the love or kindness you feel is given to you by the grace of God. It's a gift of God's grace.

CHAPTER 39

TAKING TIME TO SMELL THE ROSES

Everyone has heard the saying "Take time to smell the roses." Roses are an all-time favorite flower. They even come in all colors now, not just red, pink, and yellow. Their fragrance practically takes you to heaven and back. It's an awesome smell. They're used at weddings, anniversaries, holidays, and any occasion. Just looking at their color and taking the time to absorb their smell is totally electrifying.

Here's a story about life's average couple, but somehow something got lost in the mix.

Henry and Sheila had been married for years. Both were working forty to sixty hours each week to pay off their beautiful home, new cars, and top-of-the-line furniture. They invested their earnings in the stock market and other areas. They were giving their daughter the best life possible. At least that was what they thought. Then it happened; Henry received a call at work. While they were out shopping, his wife, daughter, and mother had been in an automobile accident. Henry suddenly stopped.

As he looked down memory lane, he remembered all the times he didn't stop and smell the roses. He remembered the time when he and his wife had planned to celebrate their first anniversary but he didn't get home until after midnight. He had forgotten all about their plans and had gone out with coworkers to celebrate his raise. He remembered the time when his daughter made all As and one B on her report card, how he was mad because she hadn't gotten all As, how she cried and ran up to her room. He remembered the time when his daughter's ninth-grade class had a father-daughter dance. He had called her with some excuse because he couldn't attend. His thoughts wouldn't stop! He remembered the time when his wife, Sheila, had planted roses in the backyard and how he hadn't even realized they were even there until they were in full bloom a year later. Every year his mother would send him birthday cards. He didn't call to thank her once. He remembered many times he had canceled plans with the family because of the next great deal or the next unbelievable change "to make a mint," as he would always say.

All these empty memories were in his past, and he couldn't do a thing about it. Henry found himself alone and empty, praying his family would survive. He experienced many moments of grief. Days went by, and then weeks passed.

He found himself hoping and praying for a miracle. He now realized how important to him his family was, not the things they had like the house, the cars, their so-called high-standing status or the rich lifestyle they lived. He knew now what was important, namely his family's recovery. His family was his life! His so-called friends, his coworkers, and his boss had not even taken a moment to call him. During this time many family members and a few friends sent cards and brought in plants and flowers. The best flowers were the roses. Yes, their smell was unbelievable. The roses were all different colors. He would smell them often. Finally, he was taking the time to smell the roses.

After a long while, his wife, daughter, and mother were discharged from the hospital. What a difficult learning experience.

Henry now drives a cute little car, not the luxury car he once drove. He has a small but comfortable home, not the million-dollar home he once had. Henry's friends say that he seems happier than he's ever been, that they would have never believed it if they had not seen it with their own eyes. Now every time they see Henry, he is with his family. Henry visits his mother every week. He finally got his life together. He lives each day as if it were his last. Not one day goes by that he doesn't stop to smell the roses.

We need to love and to take the time given to us by God to celebrate family and friends. Knowing what is important in life is also a gift from God. Sometimes we don't realize what's important until we go through difficult times.

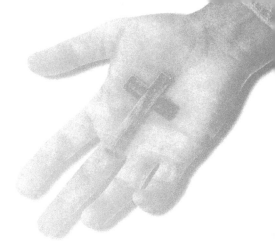

CHAPTER 40

WHAT DO YOU DO?

What do you do when everything seems to be going wrong? What do you do when it seems no one loves you? What do you do when it seems no matter how hard you try and struggle to do the right thing, all just seems to blow up in your face? What do you do when it seems you keep making the same mistake over and over again? What do you do when you actually hate yourself and feel everyone else does too? What do you do when you feel life's hardships can't get any worse? What do you do when it seems you are living this life all alone and have no one to share it with?

The answer is Jesus Christ. He is the answer to all things. John 14:6 (NJKV) says, "Jesus said, 'I am the way, the truth and the life. No one comes to the Father except through me.'"

Sometimes we have to hit rock bottom to truly pray a heart-filled prayer. Even Christians get punched, knocked down, and dragged out by life. Remember, Jesus is always there, but we must go to him. Jeremiah 29:13 (KJV) says, "Seek the Lord with all your heart and you will find him."

Jesus is waiting. Ask him into your heart today, for it's a *gift* of his grace that we are saved.

About the Author

Nancy was born in Pontotoc, Mississippi. At age twelve, she received Jesus into her heart. She doesn't consider herself to be religious, but she loves the Lord and has accepted Jesus into her heart. She believes that we all can depend on God's grace for the hope of our calling.

As a young Christian, she would assist her youth leader with programs for the Wednesday night services. She loved leading the children's choir and singing in the choir and in other groups. In years past she was an active soloist.

After her mother's death, she recorded some of her mother's original songs in her memory.

She's just a local girl, and she doesn't want to be anything else. She's a family-oriented person. Her husband, children, grandchildren, great-grandchildren, and siblings are all a big part of her life. She's just living and being happy in the grace of God.

MEMORIES

I fought hard against myself while I was writing this book. I knew I was not a scholar, but I also knew I had a powerful need to do this. When I was a teen, I often dreamed of being an English teacher. I admired my English teacher, Mrs. Pickens. She was such a light to me. I learned so much from her and loved her class. She once asked everyone in her class to raise their hand if they loved English. Two others in the classroom and I raised our hands. Many shouted, "We hate English!" I couldn't understand their lack of enthusiasm about this wonderful English book.

In my spelling class a few years earlier, I had Mr. Deline, who was an awesome teacher. I loved words, and I made all As in his class. In fact, I couldn't wait to get to his classroom to take that big test I had been preparing for.

In the second grade, I had Mrs. Lunn, which was probably the fondest of all my memories of school. I remember the joyful feeling I got just when I opened a dictionary. I still remember the smell of the new dictionary my mother had gotten me. At home I would look up words for hours and seek out their meanings.

By God's loving grace, may this book fulfill its purpose and help someone along his or her way.

Printed in the United States
By Bookmasters